William Caxton

The fifteen O's and other prayers

William Caxton

The fifteen O's and other prayers

ISBN/EAN: 9783337278571

Printed in Europe, USA, Canada, Australia, Japan

Cover: Foto ©Lupo / pixelio.de

More available books at **www.hansebooks.com**

The Fifteen O's, and other Prayers.

Printed by commandment of the Princess Elizabeth,
Queen of England and of France, and also
of the Princess Margaret, Mother
of our Sovereign Lord
the King.

By their most humble subject and servant,

William Caxton.

(circa m.cccc.xc.)

❧

Reproduced in Photo-lithography by Stephen Ayling.

Griffith and Farran,
Corner of St. Paul's Churchyard.
mdccclxix.

Dedicated to

Sir William Stirling Maxwell, Bart.,

in recognition of his patronage

and encouragement,

By his obedient servant,

Stephen Ayling.

IN prefenting, in eraĉt fac=fimile, one of the choiceſt productions of England's firſt printer, it may be as well to ſtate that the original is one of the moſt beautiful and unique ſpecimens of early Engliſh typography that is anywhere to be found. It differs in ſtyle from every other production from Carton's prefs, in that each page is furrounded by an ornamental border. The type is the fame as that uſed by him for the Virgil of 1490 : the woodcut of the crucifirion, which appears on the reverſe of the firſt leaf, erhibits conſiderable artiſtic merit, and was fub= fequently uſed by Wynkyn de Worde, and alſo by Pynſon, in ſeveral of their publications.   The original is without title, and no date is given in the colophon ; but as the Lady Elizabeth (of York) was not united to Henry (of Lancaſter), afterwards Henry vii., until 1486, this intereſting little volume, (the date of Carton's death being 1491), muſt have iſſued from the prefs between thoſe years ; moſt probably about 1490.   The volume in which it was found is in the original binding, and contains in addition, certain tracts printed by Wynkyn de Worde, and is erhibited to the public in the King's Library in Cafe viii., devoted to ſpeci= mens of the earlieſt productions of the printing prefs in

England. The original volume is in good preservation, though much cropped in the binding; the measurement being 6⅛ in. by 5 in. It was secured for the National Collection in 1851 by Sir Anthony Panizzi, at that time Keeper of the Department of Printed Books, having been purchased by him of the late Mr. Pickering for 250*l*. The prayers contained in this volume are called "The Fifteen O's," from the fact of its containing that number of prayers, with others in Latin, commencing with the exclamation O; they are common in the manuscript Horae of the 15th Century, and have frequently been reprinted both in the original Latin and in English, Caxton's version being possibly the earliest. This collection is noticed by Dr. Thomas Fuller, as being the first book of prayers tending to promote the Reformation: however this may be, they breathe a spirit of earnest devotion, and present a good illustration of the religious manuals of the period. It is more than probable that this is the first book of prayers in English issued by the followers of Wickliffe, and cannot but be interesting as having prepared the way for the great moral and spiritual changes that ended in the Reformation.

The Library of the British Museum, as might have been expected, contains the greatest number of books printed by Caxton that have ever been brought together. It includes among its treasures as many as eighty-eight pieces from his press, including fragments, and the two rare tracts discovered not long since by Mr. Winter Jones, the present Principal Librarian; of which a very interesting account may be seen in a letter addressed by that gentleman to the late Sir Henry Ellis, and printed in the papers of the Society of Antiquaries.* Of these no less than eleven are unique.

* Archæologia. Vol. xxxi. pp. 412-424.

It is fingular that out of ninety-four works enumerated in Blades' admirable "Life and Typography of William Caxton," no lefs than thirty-three are known to us only by fingle copies, or by fragments. "If," as is remarked by Mr. Blades, "more than one-third of Caxton's iffue has been nearly deftroyed, how numerous may have been the editions of which we fhall probably never learn the exiftence."

In concluding thefe brief remarks upon this unique little volume, it only remains to fay, that we are indebted to Mr. Winter Jones, for obtaining the permiffion granted by the Truftees, to reproduce this rare volume in Photo-lithography by Mr. Apling, who has done fo much to promote this modern procefs of repro-
duction; thereby bringing this bibliographic
treafure not only within the reach of
every collector of Caxton's productions, but alfo by its price,
within that, even of the
humbleft of the
lovers of old
books.

Ihesu endles swetnes of
louyng soules / O Ihesu
gostly ioye passing & ex:
ceding all gladnes and
desires. O Ihesu helthe &
tendre louer of al repentaut sinners that
likest to dwelle as thou saydest thy selfe
with the children of men / For that was
the cause why thou were incarnate / and
made man in the ende of the worlde. Ha:
ue mynde blessed Ihesu of all the sorowes
that thou suffredest in thy manhode draw
ynge nyghe to thy blessed passion / In the
whiche most holsom passion was ordey:
ned to be in thy deupne herte / By counseple
of all the hole trynyte, for the raunson of
al mankynde. Haue mynde blessed Ihesu
of al the grete dredes & anguysshes & so:
rowes that thou suffredest in thy tendre
flesshe afore thy passion on the crosse / wha
thou were betraied of thy discyple Judas

to the Jewes/whiche of famylier affecti
on that thou haddest to theym. sholde ha=
ue be thy specyal people/ After tyme that
thou haddest made thy prayer vpon the
mount of oliuete/ And swetest there to
the blood and water/ Also haue mynde
of the grete anguysshe that thou were in
whā thou were take of the false Jewes
and by fals wytnes accused. And at ihe
rusalem in the tyme of ester In the flow
ryng pougthe of thy body/ wythout tres=
pas thou receyuedest thy Jugemente of
deth vpon the crosse/ Where also thou we
re dyspoylled of thyne owne clothes/ y
scorned/ blyndfylde/ buffeted. bounde to a
pyler/ and scourged/ And wyth thornes
crowned/ and wyth a rede smyten on the
hede/ and with other innumerable peynes
thy body was all for brused and torne
For mynde of this blessed passion/ I
beseche the benygne Jhesu graunte me

afore my deth very contricyon, trewe con=
fessyon. and worthy satysfaction. And
of al my sinnes plener remyssion/amen

¶ Pater noster Aue maria

O Blessid Jhu maker of al the worl
de. that of a man may not be mesu
red/whiche closest in thy honde all the er=
the. Haue mynde of thy bitter sorow. first
& whan the Jewes fastened thy blessid
hondes to the cros. wyth blunt naples/
Also to more encrease of thy payne/they
added sorowe vpon sorowe to thy bytter
woundes. Whan they perced thy blessed
tendre feet/by cause thou woldest not ac=
corde to their wyll. And soo cruelly they
drew thy blessid body in lengthe and bre=
de to the mesure of the cros that all thy
Joyntes of thy lymmes were bothe losed
and forbroken. For mynde of thy blessed
passion/ I beseche the benygne Jhesu giue
me grace to kepe wyth me to the thy loue

O Ihesu heuenly leche haue mynde of
thy langour and blewnes of thy
woundes & sorowe that thou suffredest in
the hyght of the crosse/ whan thou were
lyfte vp fro the erthe/ that thou were all
to torne in all thy lymmes/ soo that there
was noo lymme abydynge in his right
ioynte/ soo that noo sorowe was like to
thyne· fro the sole of thy fote to the toppe
of thy hede there was no hole place/ And
yet forgetyng in maner all those greuo
us paynes/ thou purposest deuoutly & cha
ritably to thy fader for thine enimyes say
eng thus/ Fader foryeue it theim/ for they
wyte not what they done/ For this bles
sed charytable mercy that thou shew:
dest to thyne enimyes. and for mynde of
thyse bytter paynes/ graunte me/ that the
mynde of this bytter passion be to me ple
nar remyssion & foryeuenes of my sinnis

Amen/ ¶ Pater noster Aue maria

Jhesu very fredom of aungellys. pa
radys of all gostly delites/ Haue
mynde of the drede & hidous ferfulnesse
that thou suffredest whan all thyne en=
myes stode about the/ & clipped the as
wode lions smytyng the & spittynge the/
cratchyng the and many other greuous
paynes puttyng to the. For mynde of al
thise despytefull wordes. cruell betyng &
sharpe tormentes /J beseche the blessid ihe
su deliuere me from all myn enmyes bodi
ly & gostly/ And gyue me grace to haue
defence and protection of helth euerlastyn
ge/ ayest theyr wylles vnder the wynges
of thy blessid passion/ Amen

¶ Pater noster Aue maria

Jhesu blessyd myrrour of endles
clerenes/ Haue mynde of thy bles=
syd memoryall worde/ whan thou behel=
dest in the myrrour of thy ryght clere ma

geste in predestynacion of all thy chosen
soules that sholde be saued by the meryte
of thy passyon/ For mynde of the depnes
of thy grete mercy whyche thou haddest
vpon vs lost desperate sinners/ and na=
mely for the grete mercy whiche thou
shewdeste to the theef that henge on thy
ryght syde sayenge to hym thus . This
day thou shalt be wyth me in paradyse/
I praye the benygne Jhesu to shewe thy
merci to me in the hour of my deth. amen

O ❡ Pater noster Aue maria
Blessed Jhesu louable kyng. and
fende in all thyng ·Haue mynde
of the sorowes that thou haddest whan
thou hengest naked despitously vpon the
cros/ And all thy frendes and knowle=
ge stode apenst the/ of whom thou fondest
noo comforte/ But oonly of thi blessed mo
der standyng wyth the feythfully & tru
ly al the tyme of thy bitter passion/ whan

thou commaundest to thy dysciple saynt
John sayeng to her. loo womā thy sone
For mide of this passion. ҫ namely for
that swerde of sorow/the whiche that ti=
me perced the soule of thi moder/I beseche
the blessid ihesu haue compassion of me
in al tribulacions and afflictions bode=
ly ҫ gostly/ and gyue me comforte in all
my diseases/ Amen ☜ Pater nr̄. Aue

O Blessed Ihesu welle of endles py
te/ that saydest on the cros of thy
passion by inwardly affectiō of loue/ I
thurst/ that is to saye the helthe of man=
nys soule. For mynde of this blessid de=
sire. I beseche the benigne Ihu take hede to
my desire. that it maye be parfight in all
good werkes. And quenche in me the thir
ste of all fleshly loue and lust/ Amen
Pater noster Aue maria

O Blessed Ihesu swetnes of hertes
and gostli hony of soules. I beseche

the foz the bytternes of the aysel and gal
le that thou tasted and suffredest for me
in thy passion/ graunte me for to recepue
woozthely. holsomly/and deuoutly in the ho.
uz of my deth thi blessid body in the sacra
ment of the aulter/ for remedy of my sin;
nes/and comforte of my soule/ Amen

¶ Pater noster Aue maria
O Blessid Jhesu Royall strengthe
and goostly Joye/ Haue myn
de of the angupsshes/ and grete sorowes
that thou suffredest whan thou cryedest
to thy fader wyth a myghty boys/what
for the bytternes of thy deth. and also foz
the scoznyng of the Jewes sayeng thus/
O my god why haste thou forsake me/
By this paynefull angupsshe forsake
not bs in the anguisshis of our deth our
blessyd god/ Amen ¶ Pater noster aue
O Blessed Jhesu begynnyng and
endyng. liff and strengthe in euer

ry myndse/ Haue mide that fro the toppe
of thy hede to the sole of thy fote/thou suf
fredst for vs to be drowned in the wa:
ter of thy paynfull passyon. For mynde
of this grete payne· And namely for
depnes and wydenes of thy woundes/I
besech the blessed Jhu that am drowned
all in fowle sinne/tech me thy large pre
cepte ȝ comaundemēt of loue ¶/We aue

O Blessed Jhesu depnes of endles
mercy/I besech þ for the depnes of
thy woundes that wente thurgh thy ten
der flesshe/ also thy bowellis and the ma
ry of thy bones/ that thou vouchesauf to
drawe me oute of sinne/and hide me euer
after in the holes of thy woundes fro the
face of thy wrath /vnto the tyme lorde
that thy dredeful dome be passed. Amen

¶ Pater noster Aue maria

O Blessed myrrour of trouth/ token
of vnyte· ȝ louesom bonde of chari

te / Haue mynde of thyne Innumerable
peynes and woundes / wyth the whiche
fro the toppe of thy hede. to the sole of thy
fote thou were wounded / And of the
wycked Jewes thou were all to torne
and rente / And all thy body thou suf
fredeste to be rede wyth thy moost clene
blessid blode / The whiche grete sorow Je
su in thy clene virgynall body thou suf
fredest. what myghtest thou do more for
us / than thou dydest. Therfore benygne
Jhesu for the mynde of this passion wry
te al thy woudes in myn herte / wyth thy
precyous blode / that I may bothe rede in
theym thy drede and thy loue / And that
I may contynue in praysing / & in than
kynge the to my lives ende / Amen
　　　¶ Pater noster Aue maria
O Blessid Jhesu most mekest kon
　　myghtiest kyng imortal & most
victorio9. Haue mide of the sorow that

thou suffredst/ Whan al the myghtes of
thyn herte & bodi for feblenes fayled to the
Vtterly/ And thenne thou saydest encly:
nyng thyn hede thus) Now it is all done
For mynde of that anguysssh & sorowe
blessid Ihesu haue merci on me in my las
te ende. Whan my soule shall be anguys
shed and my spiryte troubled/ Amen

℣ Pater noster Aue maria

O Blessid Ihesu the onely begoten
sone of almyghty god thy fader &
shinyng likenes of his fygural substa:
unce / Haue mynde of thy meke comen:
dyng) Whan thou comendest thy spiryte
in to the hādes of thy fader. and soo thou
lostest thy bodely lyfe With a grete crypng
and With a torne body & broken hert shew
yng to Vs for our raunson the bowellis
of thy mercy/ ffor mynde of that precyo:
us deth) I beseche the kyng of the blessyd
soules. comforte me to Wythstāde the sen

ce/ the worlde & my flesshe/ that I may be
dede to the worlde/and liuyng gostly to:
warde the. And in the last hour of my de
partyng fro this worlde. receyue my sou:
le comyng to the/whiche in this life is an
outlawe or a pylgrime/ Amen

C Pater noster Aue maria

O Blessed Ihesu Verai and true plen
teuous Vyne. Haue mynde of thy
passion & habundaunt shedynge of blode/
that thou shedest most plenteuously. as
yf it had be thrust out of a rype clustre of
grapes. whan they pressed thy blessid bo:
dy as a ripe clustre Vpon the pressour of
the crosse/ And gaue Vs drynke both blo
de and water out of thy body. perced with
a knyghtes spere / soo that in thy blessed
body was not lefte a drope of blood ne of
water. thêne at last as a bundell of myr:
re thou hengest on the crosse on high/ whe
re thy tendre flesshe chaunged his colour

by cauſe the lꝗcour of thy bowellꝭ . and
ẏ mary of thy bones was dryed ꝟp. For
mynde of this byttꝛ paſſion/ ſweꝋ Iħeſu
wounde my herꝋ/and that my ſoule may
be fedde ſweꝋly wẏth water of penaunce
and teꝛes of loue bothe nyght and daye/
And good Iħeſu tourne me ħooly to the
that my herꝋ maye be euer to the a dwel;
linge place / and that my liuyng may be
euer pleſaunꝋ and acceptable . And
that the ende of my liff may be ſoo cōmen
dable /that I maye pꝛpetuelly deſerue to
prayſe the wyth all ſayntes iŋ bliſſe.
Amen.

℞ Paꝋr noſter Aue maria Credo/
        A deuouꝋ payer

O My ſouerayn lorde Iħeſu the ꝟe;
    ry ſone of almyghty god .and of
the moſt clene and glorrouſe ꝟirgyne ma
rie/ that ſuffredeſt the byttꝛ dethe for my
ſake and all mankynde ꝟpon good fry:

day/and was agayn the thirde day. I bese
che the lord haue merci vpon me/that am
a wretched sinner. But yet thy creature/
And for thy precyous passion saue me
and kepe me from al perillis bodyly & gost
ly. And specyally from all thynges that
myght torne to thy displepsir/And with
all my herte I thanke the most mercyful
lord/for the grete mercyes that thou has
te shewed me in the grete daungers that I
haue ben in/ As wel in my soule/as in
my body/ and that thy grace and endles
mercy hath euer kept me. spared me and
saued me from the hour of my byrthe in
to this tyme/I thanke the lord wyth all
my myght/ And I beseche the lord that
thy mercy may kepe me forth alway. and
I crye the mercy wyth all my hole herte
for my grete offences/ for my grete vn:
kyndenes. and for all my wretched & sin:
full life. And that I can not lede my liff

as thy seruaūt J crye the mercy/ ¶ De
us propicius esto michi peccatori / vel
peccatrici/ J thanke the also. wyth all
my herte. And my most gracious lorde
for the benefayttes ⁊ grace that thou ha
ste peuen me largely in this worlde afo;
re many other creatures. whiche haue a
thousande tymes deserued better than J/
But moost gracious lorde J wote and
knowleche verily/ that all it cometh of
the. wherfore wyth all my herte J thanke
the/ And alle the worship the prysing
and the thanke be to the. and to none o;
ther/ Non nobis dñe non nobis. sed no
mini tuo da gloriam/ ¶ Adonay dñe
deus magne rex admirabilis/qui dedisti
salutem in manus sancte Birginis/ et
per Berum .et per Biscera dulcissime ma
tris tue / et per illud dulcissimū corpus
tuū quod ex ea sumpsisti/exaudi preces
meas/ ⁊ imple desiderium meū in bonum

et libera me ab omni tribulacione ꝛ an=
guſtia ꝛ a morte ſubitania. et ab oibus
inſidiis. ꝛ ab oibus michi nocentibus/
ꝛ a linguis iniqnis ꝛ dolofis/ et ab oibʒ
malis pꝛeſentibus. pꝛeritis .ꝛ futuris⸖
Amen/ ⸿ pſalm9/ Dñe dñs ñr/ cũ
Glia pꝛi. Sicut erat
⸿ Ab inimicis nꝛis defende nos ꝛpe/
Afflictionem noſtram benignus vide.
Dolorem coꝛdis noſtri reſpice clemens
Peccata populi tui pius indulge. Ora
ciones nꝛas pius eꝛaudi/ Fili dei viui
miſerere nobis . Hic et impꝛpetuũ nos
cuſtodire digneris ꝛpe/ Eꝛaudi nos/eꝛ
audi/ eꝛaudi nos ꝛpe/   Oraco
⸿ Infirmitatem nꝛam qͫs dñe propi
cius reſpice ꝛ mala omnia que iuſte me
remur omnium ſanctoꝛũ tuoꝛ interceſ
ſione auerte. Per cꝛiſtũ dñm nꝛm/amen

⸿ A deuote praꝑ

Jhesu for thy holy name/ and for thy bitter passyon/Saue vs fro synne and shame / and endles dampnacōn/ And bryng vs to thy blisse that neuer shall haue ende swete Jhesu amen·And graunte vs of thy grace that to the honour and worship of thy holy name, to the laude & prœysing of thy blessyd moder and virgyne, our lady saynte marie. And to the prouffyt of our moder holy chirche we may do our duete and homage eche wyth other, and for other. swete Jhesu amen /

Ost dere lorde and saupour swete Jhesu/ I beseche thy moost curtoys goodnes and benygne fauour/ to be to me most wretched creatur fauourable lorde, protectour, kepʳ, and defender/ and in al necessitees & nedes/ be to me shelde & protection/ ayenst al myne

emptes bodely and gostely) Mercifull
Jhesu I haue none other truste. hope/ ne
socour . but in the allonely my dere lorde
swete Jhesu/the whiche of thy Infenyte
goodnes madest me of nought/like Bry
to thy most excellent ymage/ And whan
I was loste. by my firste fader Adams
sinne. wyth thy precious blode dere lord
thou redemest me/ And sithen euer day
ly most graciously wyth thy gyftes of
grace most louyngly thou fedest me. gra
unte me therfore my most dere lord and
sauyour to drede the /and loue the . abo
ue all thyng in this present liff/ and af
ter in ioye and blisse wythoute ende swe
te Jhesu/ Amen

O Blessid lady moder of Jhesu and
Virgyne inmaculate/that art wel
of comforte and moder of mercy. singu
ler helper to all that trust to the/ be now
gracyous lady medyatryce and meane

Bnto thy blessid sone our sauyour Jhesu
for me/ that by thy intercessions J may
optepne my despres. euer to be your ser
uaunt in all humplite/ And by the hel
pe and socour of al holy saynctes herafter
in perpetuell iope euer to liue wyth the/
Amen /

¶ To the propre angell
a deuoute prayer

O Gloryous angell to whom our
Blessyd lord of his most mercyful
grace hath taken me to kepe. To the J
sinful creature crye and calle with herte
ly mynde/ besechyng the euer to be singu
ler comforte to me in all my nede/ Suf
fre me neuer to be ouercome wyth temp
tacyon or synfull dede/ But helpe me/ that
by grace J may euer in vertuous liuyn
ge procede/ At the hour of my deth be pre
sent/ that my goostly enmy.in me haue
noo power/ And after brynge me to

eliſſe / wohere euer woyth the I may liue/
and prayſe our ſauiour. Amen/ ¶ R̄
¶ Spem in alium nũquam habui. pꝛe
ter in te deus iſrael/ Qui iraſceris et pꝛo
picius eris / et omnia peccata hominũ
In tribulacione dimittis. ¶ Verſus
Domine deus cæli et terre reſpice ad hu
militatem nr̃am. Qui iraſceris et q̃ c̃
Gloria p̃ri. In tribulacõe/ Sit noiē
dr̃i. Ex hoc nunc/q̃ c̃   Oremus

Rotector in te ſperancium deus
ſine quo nichil eſt validũ nichil
ſanctũ multiplica ſuper nos mi
ſericordiam tuã/Et te rectore/te duce/ ſic
tranſeam9 per bona temporalia. Et non
amittamus eterna/ p xp̃m dr̃m nr̃z

¶ Ad ſcãm Trinitatem
Omine deus omnipotens pater
et fili9 et ſpũs ſcũs/ da michi fa
mulo tuo.N. Vel famulę tue.N
Victoriam contra oēs homines / et ſuper

oms̄ qui michi cupiũt nocere/ Et non
possint michi nocere/nec cōtradicere/sed
dirigatur virt9 eoꝝ et cōsiliũ iɴ bonũ
Et tu deus oĩpotens sis fortitudo mee
ꝗ refugiũ meũ.ꝗ clipeus defēsionis mea
et ignis iextinguibilis/ ꝗ turris imobi
lis fortitudinis ꝗ protcciois mee/quati
nus dispergāt oēs aduersarij mei ꝗ ini
mici· Deus abraham.deus Isaac/deus
Jacob/deus oĩm bene viuēciũ/libera me
famulũ tuũ.N. vel famulā tuā.N. ab
oĩbus peccatis meis/angustiis/ꝗ tribu
lacionibus/necessitatibus/ et periculis/
et da michi robur fortitudinē/et perseue
rānciã iɴ bonũ/et sermonē rectũ/et bene
sonātē iɴ os meũ. Et placita sit oĩa ver
ba mea.Vultus/ et opera mea oĩbus ho;
minibꝫ me videntibus.ꝗ audientibꝫ Et
iueuiã grām et auxliũ in oĩbus peticio
nibꝫ meis/Propheta clamat/apostolus
dicit/ cristus in se confitentes saluat/

✠ criſtus vincit ✠ criſtus regnat
criſtus imperat dignetur me eſſe triū
phatorem omnium aduerſariorū meorū
et non timebo quid faciat michi homo/
Deus in nomine tuo ſaluū me fac/ et
libera me ab oibus hoſtiis viſibilibz et
inuiſibilibus. et concede michi ſpacium
vere penitecie/Et in nomine tuo exhibeā
et impetrem aliquid honoris et pomoci
onis huius terreni ſeculi.   Dñe Iheſu
xpe fili dei viui qui in cruce ſuſpendi vo
luiſti/et lancea latus perforari permiſiſ
ti/ et de tuo precioſo ſanguine me rede
miſti/et tres pueros de camino ignis li
beraſti/ Sydrac/Miſaac/et Abdenago
et ſuſannam de falſo crimine conſeruaſ
ti/et Danielem de lacu leonum liberaſti
Ita per hec verba libera me famulū tu
um.N.vel famulam tuā.N.ab omni
aduerſitate corporis et anime/et omni o
pere malo preſenti et futuro·Amen

In nomine patris et filij et spiritus
sancti.amen ℂ Pater noster / Aue
maria. ℂ Psalmi
Deus in noîe tuo saluū me fac/q̄ c̄
Deus misereatur n̄ri et b̄ndicat nob̄
De profūdis clamaui ad te d̄ñe/
Uoce mea ad d̄ñm clamaui/Boce
Ad te leuaui oculos meos,/qui h̄itas
Leuaui oculos meos in montes
Beati omnes qui timent d̄ñm
ℂ Jh̄us autem transiens per medium
illoꝛ ibat. ℂ Oraco ad patrem
Omine s̄ce pater omnipotens
eterne deus/in illa s̄ca custodia
et memoria in qua comendasti
gloriocissimum spiritū filij tui d̄ñi n̄ri
Jh̄su cristi/quando misisti eū de celis ad
terram/et in illa sancta custodia et me-
moria in qua respondisti et cōmendasti
gliosā matrē et persona filij tui existēs
in b̄ndicta cruce. quā cōmendasti Joh̄i

protegat et defendat ab omnibus inimi͞
cis meis Visibilibus et inuisibilibus
Sancte michael defende me in prelio.in
placito/et letigio sedendo/stando/iacendo
edendo/bibendo.Vigilado/sompniando/lo
quendo.cogitando/et in oībus locis ope͞
ra mea faciendo/ Vt non peream in isto
seculo/neqz in tremendo iudicio/ Archā
gele cristi michael / per graciam quam
meruisti te deprecor per dominū nostrum
Jhm cristū Vnigenitum filium dei.Vt e͞
ripias me hodie et in omni tempore a la
queo mortis/ et ab omnibus periculis
corporis et aīe/Sancte michael/Sanc
te gabriel. Sancte Raphael · et omnes
sancti angeli dei succurrite michi/Pre͞
cor et supplico Vos omnes Virtutes celo
rū/ Vt michi famulo Vestro/ Vel famule
Vestre/per summam dei potenciam sitis
michi in auxiliū/ Vt nullus inimicus
michi nocere poterit iperpetuū/Amen /

¶ Alia Oracio ad dominū

Domine ihu xpe fili dei viui deus
olpotens rex glorie. qui mundū
proprio sanguine redemisti / Exaudi me
miserū peccatorem / Vel miseram pecca
tricem quotidie peccantem / et in peccatis
iacentem / Tibi soli peccaui / tibi xpe con
fiteor. ego miserrimus. Vel miserima om
nium creaturax peccator / Vel peccatrix
peccaui coram te dñe et coram angelis
tuis / in verbis. factis / delectacōnibz / con
sensibz. et cogitacōnibus malis et luxu
riosis / Item in superbia / Inuidia / Ira / ac
cidia. auaricia gula. et luxuria / Infelix
nimis ego sum. Innumerabilia sunt de
licta mea / Olpotens deus miserere mei
peccoris. Vel mee peccatricis / Veniam pe
to coram te dñe et coram angelis tuis
de vniuersis peccatis meis preteritis pre
sentibus et futuris / Domine deus qui
fons es pietatis et misericordie / propici9

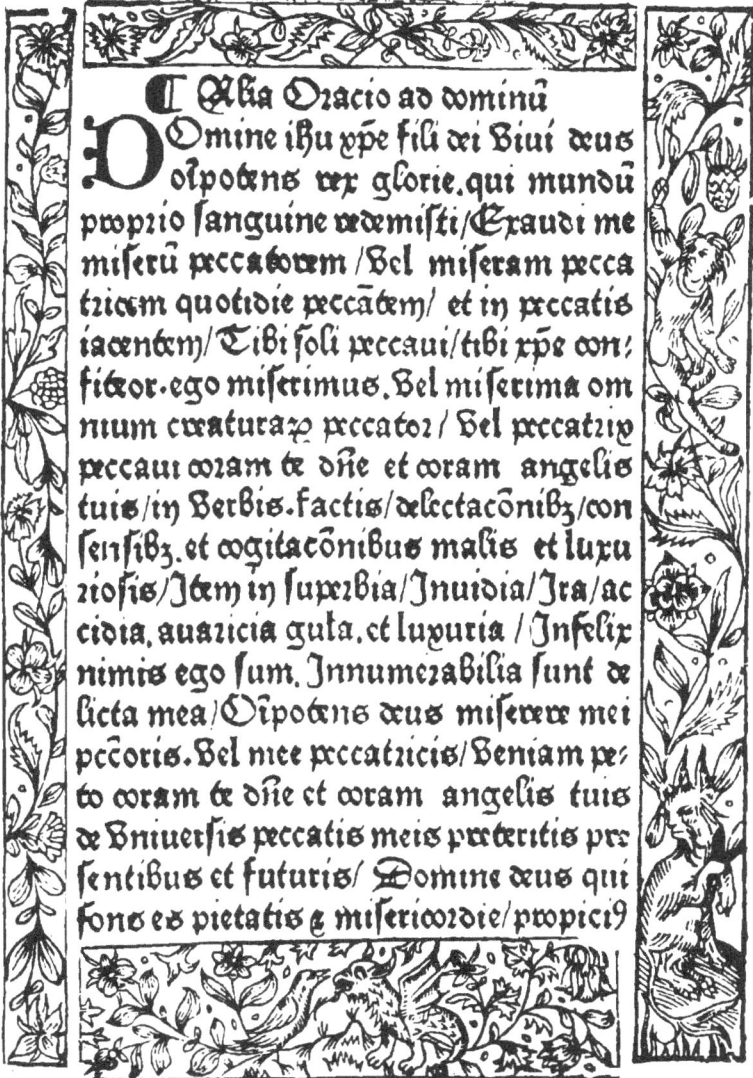

esto michi peccatori. Bel peccatrici. Da
michi ſpacium Bere penitencie / per quã
deleam oĩa peccata mea / quia neſcio Bbi
fugiam niſi ad te deus meus / quia tu es
Bita mea et reſurreptio mortuoꝝ ! Ora
ꝑ me mater miſericordie / Orate pro me
peccatore. Bel peccatrice omes ſancti an
geli et archangeli. Throni et dominaci⸗
ones. Principatus et poteſtates. Bir⸗
tutes. cherubin atqꝜ ſeraphin / Orate pro
me patriarche omes / et ſancti prophete /
Orate pro me peccatori. Bel peccatrice
omes ſancti apoſtoli martires et confeſ
ſores. Orate pro me omes ſancte Birgi
nes mulieres et Bidue ſancte / atqꝜ om⸗
nes ſancti et ſancte dei. Et deus illumi⸗
net faciem ſuã ſuper me miſerum pecca⸗
torem. Bel peccatricem / et miſeriatur mei
et tocius populi criſtiani / Amen!

¶ Pater noſter Aue maria
¶ Oracio ſancte crucis

Ignum sancte crucis defendat
me a malis preteritis presentibz
et futuris interioribus et exteri
oribus/ ✝ Signum sancte crucis a per
secusione diaboli et oium inimicorum me
orum liberet me/ ✝ Hoc signaculo proster
nantur omnes aduersarij mei et fugi=
ant/ ✝ Per hoc signu sancte crucis a
periculis mūdi liberet me dūs. ✝ Bene
dictio dei patris cum angelis suis sit su
pra me/ ✝ Benedictio Ihu xpi cum apo
stolis suis sit supra me/ ✝ Benedictio
proteccio/et sanctifica cio dei cum virtu
te misteriozp sancti euangelij sit supra
me. ✝ Benedictio dominice incarnacio
nis et sancte natiuitatis. circumcisiōis
beate passionis. veneranda resurrectio=
nis / admirabilis ascencionis et gra=
cia sancti spiritus paracliti. et signū sce
crucis ✝ sit super me/infra me/circa me
iuxta me/ante me. et post me in ōnibus

operibus meis/ ✠ benedictio beate mari
e/et sco₂ patriacha₂um/ prophetay. apo
stolo₂/martiru/confesso₂/ Birginu. et
Biduay continenciu sit supra me. Et
comendo corpus meu et aiam sancte tri
nitati Bt custodiat me hic et in futuro/
✠ Erux tua diie Jhu xpe fit signu sa
lutis mee.per quam redimere dignatus
es me/Adiutor.protector/consolator. de
fenso₂.gubernator/a illuminator sis me
us/diie deus. ✠ benedictio sancte trini
tatis me custodiat/foueat/protegat/et de
fendat ab oibus malis/ et confortet me
in omni opere bono Bt hic et ineternum
saluari merear/Amen   ℂ Psalm9
Nclina diie aurem tuā et exaudi
me/quoniam inops et pauper su
ego/Custodi aiam meā quonia scūs
sum/saluum fac seruu tuū deus meus
speratem in te/Miserere mei diie qm ad
te clamaui tota die.letifica aiam serui

tui.quoniam ad te domine annimam me
am leuaui/ Quoniam tu dñe suauis e
mitis/ꝗ multe misericordie omnibꝫ in
uocantibus te/ Auribus percipe oracio
nem meam/et intende voci deprecacioîs
mee. In die tribulaĉonis mee clamaui
ad te. quia exaudisti me. Non est simi
lis tui iŋ diis dñe/ et non est scdm opera
tua. Omnes gentes quascũꝗ fecisti/
venient et adorabũt coram te dñe. et glo
rificabũt nomeŋ tuũ. Q ꝫ magnus es
tu et faciens mirabilia/ tu es deus solꝰ
Deduc me dñe iŋ via tua. et ingrediar
in veritate tua/letetur cor meũ vt time
at nomen tuũ/ Confitebor tibi dñe de
us iŋ toto corde meo . et glorificabo no
men tuũ ineternũ/ Quia misericordia
tua magna est super me/et eruisti aĩam
meam ex inferno inferiori / Deus inꞽ
qui insurrexerũt super me/ et sinagoga
potenciũ quesierũt aĩam meaŋ/et non

proposuerunt. & in conspectu suo/ Et tu
dñe deus miserator et misericors paci/
ens et multe misericordie et verax .Res
pice in me et miserere mei/ da imperium
puero tuo.et saluū fac filium ancille tue
Fac mecū signū in bono Vt videāt qui
oderunt me et confundantur/ qm tu dñe
adiuuisti me/et consolatus es me/ Glo
ria ptī/ Sicut/ Kyriel rpel/ kyriel/ pa
ter nr.aue maria. Et ne nos/ Adorem9
crucis signaclm/ Per quod salutis sūp
simus sacramentum) Oremus

Sanctifica quesum9 dñe famlū
tuū/vel famkam tuā signaculo
sce crucis/ Vt fiat obstaculū con
tra seua iacula inimicorum oīm/ defende
me per lignum sctm tuū et precium iusti
sanguinis in quo me redemisti/ Qui cū
deo patre et spiritu sancto viuis per om
nia secula seculorz. Amen

℡ Itm Oracio ad dñm

Omine Ihesu xpe apud me sis
Bt me defendas. intra me sis Bt
me reficias / circa me sis Bt me
conserues/ante me sis ut me custodias/
subtus me sis ut me subleues/supra me
sis Bt me larga dextra tua benedicas
Simplex et trine me conserues sine fi=
ne/ In noie patris et filij/ et spus sancti
amen/ ✚ Sancte Michael esto michi
lorica/ ✚ Sancte gabriel esto michi ga
lea. ✚ Sancte Raphael esto michi scu
tu. ✚ Sce Uriel esto michi defensor ✚
Sce cherubin esto michi sanitas ✚ / sac
te seraphin esto michi Beritas/Et om=
nes sancti angeli et archangeli me cus
todiant. protegant/ et defendant.et ad Bi
tam eternam me perducant/Amen
Dulcissime Ihesu inspira cordi me
o tuu sanctissimum amorem, mu
di contemptum. peccati odium · celes=
tis patrie desiderium/ perseueranciam

penitencie/quam nec morbus impediat
donec tua miseracio eam perducat ad ef=
fectum. amen.

℩ Ad Crucem

Quicquid inimicus meus alliga=
Querit in me. per suám iniquitatem
ypsus filius dei vini dignetur .obsoluere
per sua resurrectionem. O pie crucifixe
redemptor oim populorum. qui pro salute
generis humani ab impiorum manibus
mortis supplicium pertulisti. propter no
men sanctu tuu/et per merita et interces
siones beatissime genitricis tue marie et
omniu scorum tuorum propicius esto michi
peccatori/vel peccatrici. et exaudi preces
meas secundu multitudine misericordie
tue/Omnis terra adoret te deus et psal=
lat tibi. Psalmu dicat nõi tuo/℩ Oro

Deus qui per crucem passiois tue
nos redemisti. et sanguinem preci
ocissimu fudisti/salua nos per lignum

sanctæ crucis/ quam nos in honore no=
minis tui deuotissimi adoramus/ Qui
viuis & regnas cu deo pre i vnitate spi
ritus sci deus/ per oia scla sclo℞. amen

¶ Item alia oracio ad dñm

Ita viuencium ypce ab iniqua et
subitanea morte libera me. Be=
ray vita ypce a terribili et subita
nia morte erue me/ ypce salus vite ab an
gustiis subitance mortt protege me/ qui
plasmasti me et precioso sanguine tuo
redemisti me/ ne paciaris preuentu subi
tance mortt/ vitam quam dedisti michi
vllo modo finiri/ sed humane condicios
figmentum intuens. custodi me vigi=
lantem/ tuere me dormientem/ conserua
me viuente. vita imortalis ypce. pay hic
sal9 hic/ Trinitas sca me famulu tuu
vel famulam tuam sine intermissione
custodi. Amen/ Kirieleyson/ ypcekyson

kinelepſon/ ℭPater noſter. Aue maria
Et ne nos. Sed libera nos/ ℭOrem9
Omnipotens ſempiterne deus non
me permittas perire/ quia tua cre
atura ſum/ſed concede michi ſpaciuȝ Bi
te Biuendi/ Btante diem exitus mei per
Beram penitenciam tibi placere merear
ℭPer domimū noſtrum Jhm criſtum fi
lium tum qui tecum Biuit et regnat in
Bnitate ſpiritus ſancti deus/ ℭPer oīa
ſecula ſeculozum/ Amen

ℭ Oracio contra temptacōnes
Eus qui contritozuȝ non deſpi
cis gemitum/ et merencium nō
ſpernis affectum/Adeſto preci
bus meis qua pietati tue pro tribulact;
one mei.N. offero/Jmplorans Bt me cle
menter reſpicias/ et ſolito pietatis tue
intuitu tribuas/Bt quicquid contra me
diabolice atqȝ humane moliũtur aduer;

sitates/ad nichilum redigas/et consilio
misericordie tue allidas/quatenus nul;
lis aduersitatibz lesus. Bel lesa. Sed ab
omni tribulacõne et angustia liberatus
Bel liberata gracias tibi in ecclesia tua
referro consolatus Bel consolata/Per do;
minum nostrũ Ihesum cristũ /xc̃

℣ Contra mortalitatem hoĩm

Per signũ tau   a peste expedimie
litera nos Ihesu. Hic est titu lus
triumphalis/ Ihesus nazaren9
Rex iudeorum/ Cristus Benit in pace/de
us homo factus est Ihesus amen,/ Sanc
te deus/ Sancte fortis. Sãcte et inmor
talis/ Agnus dei qui tollis peccata mũ
di miserere nobis. Signatum est super
nos Bultus tui domine. dedisti leticiam
in corde meo.   Signium salutis pone
domine in domibus in quibus habita;

mus / et non permittas introire angelū
percucientem de celo. ℞ Pone signum
tuum domine et protege nos/et non erit
in nobis plaga nocens / ℂ Versus
Miserere nostri domine miserere/℞ Vt
a peste epidimie liberemur. Oremus
Vsita nos quesumus domine et ha
bitacōnem istam ab omnibus in=
sidiis inimici. tuere et procul eas repel=
le / Angeli tui sacti nos inhabitantes
in ea/pace custodiant·et benedicant sem
per. et nos famuli tui ab omni pestilen=
cia subitania et improuisa morte libere=
mur/Per cristum dñm nostrū.

℃ Sequitur oracio de
beato rege Henrico

Rex henricus sis amic9/nob iŋ āgustia
Cui9 per nos a nece/saluemur perpetua
lāpas morp/spes egrorp/feres medicaia

Sis tuozp famulozp/ductor ad celeſtia
Pax i terra nõ ſit guerra. orb p cõfinia
Virt9 creſcat et feruescat caritas p oīa
Nõ ſudoze/vel doloze/moriamur ſubito
Sed viuam9 ꝓ plaudam9 cœl ſine terio
℀ Verſus Ora ꝓ nobis deuote rex ħen
rica/ ℟ Vt per te cuncti ſupratı ſunt
inimici. ℀ Oĕo/   Oremus

Reſta queſum9 omnipotens et
miſericors deus / Vt qui deuotiſſi
mi regis ħenrici merita miraculis ful
gencia. pie mentis affectu recolimus in
terzis. eius et omniū ſcozp tuozp inter
ceſſionibus ab omni peſte/febre. morbo
ac inprouiſa morte. ceterisqz eruamur
malis/ꝗ gaudia ſempiterna adipiſci me
reamur.Per ꝓpm dīm noſtrum/amen/

℀ Ad ſanctū Rochum   Ant
O quam magnificum eſt nomē
tuum beate Rocħe/qui tuis interceſſioni
bus multitudinem languencium noſtı

faiuare/et ab omnibʒ nomen tuū glori=
ofum cōmemorantibus. ɬ pwpicium ey
hibere/Beni et falua nos a morbo epide=
mie et aeris ɬmpꝛiem nobis concede.
℄ Verfus/ Ora pw noᵬis fancɬ Po=
cɬe/℞ Vt digni efficiamur promiffio=
nibus ꝑpi/Oꝛemus/ ℄ Oꝛacio
Omnipotens fempiterne deus qui
meritis ɬ pꝛecibus ᵬeatiffimi ro
chi confefforis tui quandam peſ
ɬem generalꝑm reuocafti/pꝛefta fupplici
bus tuis/Vt qui pw fimili peſte reuocan
da ad ipfum fuᵬ tua confidunt fiducia/
ipfius gloriofi confefforis tui precami=
ne/aᵬ ipfa peſte epidemie/ɋ aᵬ omni per
turbacōne liᵬerentuꝛ. Per dm̄ noſtrū
Jhm̄ xp̄m filium tuū qui ɬcū/ɋ c̄

℄ To euery criſten creature able to re
ceyue pardon/ fayeng this antheme and

colette folowynge. wythin the chirche or
chircheyerde/is graunted for euery cryſ:
ten creature there beryed xl. dayes of par
dom/and xiij. lentes)

A Vete fideles omes anime/in ſca
dei pace requieſcite/qui vos rede
mit precioſo ſuo ſaguine. vobis
dignetur miſereri. penaſq3 veſtras mi:
nuere. aicq3 veſtre quaꝝ corpora. ſunt
hic et vbiq3 ſepulta. et anime oium fide
lium defunctoꝛ. per dei miam requieſcat
in pace perpetua/Amen/Oro/ Oremus

O Iſecre dne per tuam glorioſam
reſurrectionem aibus oium fide
liu defunctoꝛ. et miſerere aibus
illis/que apud te ſingularem no habent
interceſſorem. quibus non eſt conſolacō
neq3 ſpes vlla i tormetis ſuis. niſi quod
facte ſut ad pmaginem tuā. Parce do:
mine parce et defende plaſma tuum in
eis. et ne des honorem nominis tui

peccamur alteri. Opus manuũ tuaꝛ
ne despicias in eis / sed porrige eis ma-
num tuã dexteram/et libera eas de Intol
lerabilibus penis ꝫ angustiis inferni.et
perduc eas ad societatem ciuium super-
norum propter nomen sanctũ tuum Ihe
sus. Amen.   ¶ Requiescant in pace
𝕬𝕸𝕰𝕹

¶ Thiese prayers tofore wreton ben en
prited bi the comaundementes of the mo
ste hye ꝫ vertuous pryncesse our liege la
di Elizabeth by the grace of god Quene
of Englonde ꝫ of Fraũce. ꝫ also of the
right hye ꝫ most noble pryncesse Marga
rete Moder vnto our souerayn lorde the
kyng/ꝫ c̃

¶ By their most humble subget and
seruaũt William Caxton

www.ingramcontent.com/pod-product-compliance
Lightning Source LLC
Chambersburg PA
CBHW021437090426
42739CB00009B/1523